W9-AZO-980

ADAM AND EVE

THE BIBLE STORY

ADAPTED AND ILLUSTRATED BY
WARWICK HUTTON

MARGARET K. McELDERRY BOOKS
NEW YORK

This b... for Nell

Copyright © 1987 by Warwick Hutton

Margaret K. McElderry Books
Macmillan Publishing Company
866 Third Avenue
New York, NY 10022
Collier Macmillan Canada, Inc.

The original pictures for *Adam and Eve: The Bible Story* are watercolor paintings.
Composition by Linoprint Composition Co., Inc., New York, New York
Printed and bound by Toppan Printing Company in Japan

First Edition
10 9 8 7 6 5 4 3 2

Library of Congress Cataloging-in-Publication Data

Hutton, Warwick.
Adam and Eve.

Summary: Retells the Biblical story of God's
creation of the world and the subsequent disobedience
of Adam and Eve.
1. Adam (Biblical figure)—Juvenile literature.
2. Eve (Biblical figure)—Juvenile literature.
3. Creation—Juvenile literature. 4. Bible stories,
English—O.T. Genesis. [1. Adam (Biblical figure)
2. Eve (Biblical figure) 3. Creation. 4. Bible
stories—O.T.] I. Title.
BS580.A4H88 1987   222'.1109505   86-27690
ISBN 0-689-50433-0

In the beginning God created the heaven and the earth, and the earth was without form, and darkness was upon the face of the deep. And the spirit of God moved upon the face of the waters.

And God said, "Let there be light," and there was light. And God saw the light that it was good, and God divided the light from the darkness. And God called the light Day, and the darkness He called Night.

And God said, "Let there be a firmament in the midst of the waters."

And God made the firmament and called the firmament Heaven.

And God said, "Let the waters under the heaven be gathered together unto one place, and let the dry land appear." And God called the dry land Earth, and the gathering together of the waters He called Seas. And the earth brought forth grass, and herb yielding seed after its kind, and trees yielding fruit.

And God made two great lights, the greater light to rule the day, and the lesser light to rule the night; He made the stars also. And God set them in the firmament of the heaven to give light upon the earth.

And the Lord God formed man of the dust of the ground, and breathed into his nostrils the breath of life, and man became a living soul.

And the Lord God planted a garden eastward in Eden, and there He put the man He had formed. And out of the ground the Lord God made to grow every tree that is pleasant to the sight and good for food; He also put the tree of life and the tree of knowledge of good and evil in the midst of the garden. And the Lord God commanded the man, saying, "Of every tree in the garden you may freely eat. But of the tree of knowledge of good and evil, you must not eat, for the day you eat thereof you shall surely die."

And out of the ground the Lord God formed every
beast of the field, and every bird of the air, and brought
them to Adam to see what he would call them, and
whatsoever Adam called every living creature, that was
the name thereof.

And the Lord God caused a deep sleep to fall upon Adam and he slept, and God took one of his ribs. And the rib, which the Lord God had taken from man, He made into a woman, and He brought her unto the man.

And they were both naked, the man and his wife,
and were not ashamed.

Now the serpent was more subtle than any beast of the field which the Lord God had made. And he said to the woman, "Has God said you shall not eat of every tree of the garden?"

And the woman said to the serpent, "We may eat the fruit of the trees of the garden, but of the fruit of the tree which is in the middle of the garden, God has said, 'You shall not eat of it, lest you die.'"

And the serpent said to the woman, "Surely you shall not die. For God knows that the day you eat from it, then your eyes shall be opened, and you shall be as gods, knowing good and evil."

And when the woman saw that the tree was good for food and pleasant to the eyes, and a tree to be desired to make one wise, she took one of its fruits, and did eat, and gave one to her husband, and he did eat.

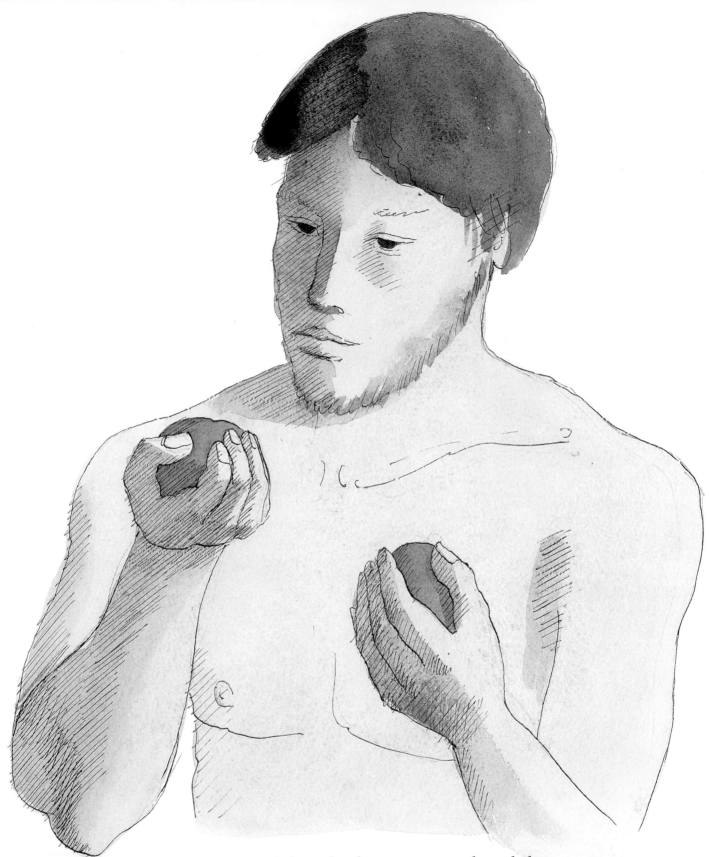

And the eyes of them both were opened, and they
knew that they were naked, and they sewed fig leaves
together, and made themselves aprons.

And they heard the voice of the Lord God, walking in the garden in the cool of the day, and Adam and his wife hid themselves from the presence of the Lord God amongst the trees of the garden

And the Lord God called to Adam, and said to him, "Where are you?"

And Adam said, "I heard your voice in the garden, and I was afraid because I was naked, and I hid myself."

And God said, "Who told you that you were naked? Have you eaten of the tree that I commanded you should not eat?"

And the man said, "The woman you gave to be with me, she gave me fruit from the tree, and I did eat."

And the Lord God said to the woman, "What is this that you have done?"

And the woman said, "The serpent beguiled me, and I did eat."

And the Lord God said to the serpent, "Because you have done this, you are cursed above all cattle, and above every beast of the field. Upon your belly shall you go, and dust shall you eat all the days of your life."

To the woman He said, "In sorrow shall you bring forth children."

And to Adam He said, "Because you have listened to the voice of your wife, and have eaten of the tree of which I commanded you that you should not eat, cursed is the ground for your sake. In sorrow shall you eat of it all the days of your life. For dust you are and unto dust shall you return."

And Adam called his wife's name Eve, because she was the mother of all living.

For Adam and his wife the Lord God made coats of skins and clothed them. The Lord God sent them forth from the garden of Eden to till the ground from whence they were taken.

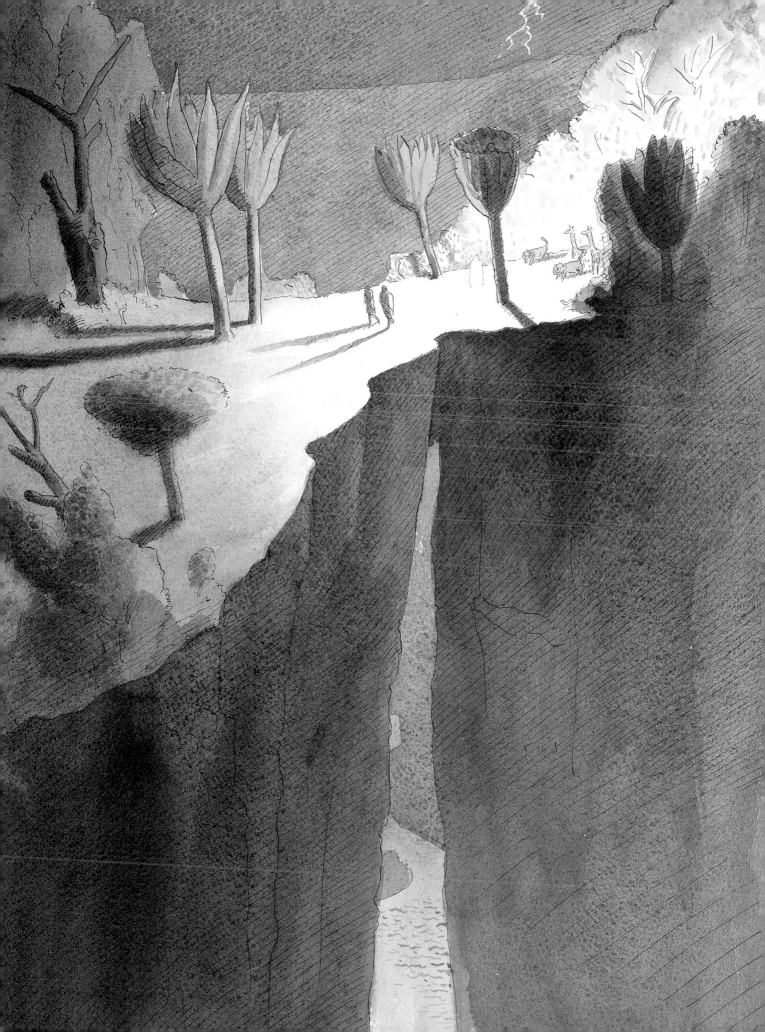

So He drove out the man and the woman from the garden of Eden, and He placed at the east of the garden cherubims and a flaming sword to guard the tree of life.